IT'S TIME TO RHYME

{314}

IT'S TIME TO RHYME

Poems for Kids of All Ages

SHOBHA THAROOR SRINIVASAN

Illustrated by Priya Kuriyan

ALEPH BOOK COMPANY
An independent publishing firm
promoted by ***Rupa Publications India***

First published in India in 2022
by Aleph Book Company
7/16 Ansari Road, Daryaganj
New Delhi 110 002

ISBN: 978-93-91047-60-3

3 5 7 9 10 8 6 4

For sale in the Indian subcontinent only.

Printed at India

For Mrinalini, Shai, Eliseo, Ximena,
Kahaani, and all the readers to come.
May poetry always be a part of your life.

Contents

Author's Note

In this book, I guide readers through various poetic forms, from sonnets in iambic pentameter to limericks and acrostics and villanelles, by introducing each type of poem in the style that explains the rules for the form. I then follow it with an original poem on a relatable subject so that the learning is fun for young readers. The book is, therefore, both a poetry reader and an instructional text that should serve to dispel fears of rhyme schemes and rigid structure that children sometimes have about poetry.

My intent is to explain various poetic forms through a method that allows readers to truly examine poetry in a way that is both engaging and easy to understand. My hope is that by including the example poems on subjects that resonate (like the trials of homework, the delectable joy of ice cream flavours, the thrill of junk food) children will be drawn to composing poems as well.

As readers of the American edition have said,

these poems are 'fun, inventive, and deceptively simple; they hide some important and difficult ideas'. I hope that teachers will appreciate the book and that it makes their job of explaining unfamiliar poetic forms much easier. And I hope that children will grasp poetic forms and literary terms much better because fun rhymes have been utilized to attract and keep their attention. I have used universally appealing themes of family, home, love, food, and friendship in the poems written for the second half of the book.

Whether you're a young reader interested in verse, a parent looking for a fun-filled way to explore poetry with your children, or a rhyme-enthused teacher looking for a unique poetry text, I hope that this is your go-to book to learn about the foundations of poetry.

How many lines in a limerick?
What makes a poem really tick?
Let's practice with English, recite and rehearse,
How words become stanzas, then stories in verse!
Gerunds are verbs that end with an 'ing'
Like you're 'sitting' and 'looking' and also 'reading'.
The Grawlix is strange. Like a growler it sounds.
But it is just @#$%&!'! A string of symbols that pounds!
The letters 'o-u-g-h' six ways turn my tongue,
Dough, rough, borough, through, bough, and bought can be sung.
Synecdoche is when a part stands for the whole:
Like 'wheels' for car, 'crown' for king, and salad 'leaves' in a bowl.
So let's turn the page and take poems to new heights.
I'll share POETIC FORMS and make the rhythms real tight.
I'll show you how far the English language will go,
To make learning fun and rhyming more so!

Sonnet in Iambic Pentameter

The sonnet is just a simple poem.
Its length is predetermined at the start.
Fourteen lines in total, not a long tome,
The Octave's eight, the Sestet's six apart.
The first eight lines may rhyme quite easily.
The next six lines may change repeatedly.
Though the meter can vary, I'll show you,
Some sonnets have five long beats through and through.
Milton, Dante, and the great bard as well,
With thoughtful words of life and death did tell.
This form they used to express sentiment.
They spoke of love, and war, and merriment.
The sonnet is an interesting find,
Just fourteen lines to speak what's on your mind!

When Mummy Was Away

I packed my own lunch, when Mummy was out,
With sweets and treats, since she wasn't about.
Took out the salad, threw carrots away,
Put in some cookies, a packet of Lays.
Filled up my thermos with sweet Seven-Up,
Joyfully dreaming of 'fizz' in my cup.
Pulled out my sandwich. Added some cake.
This was a great lunch. I made no mistake.
But something went very wrong with my plan;
You don't want to look in the garbage can...
Through recess, I lay on the ground in pain
I'll never try packing my lunch again.
All that sugar gave me a tummy ache
Junk food for lunch is a major mistake!

Haiku

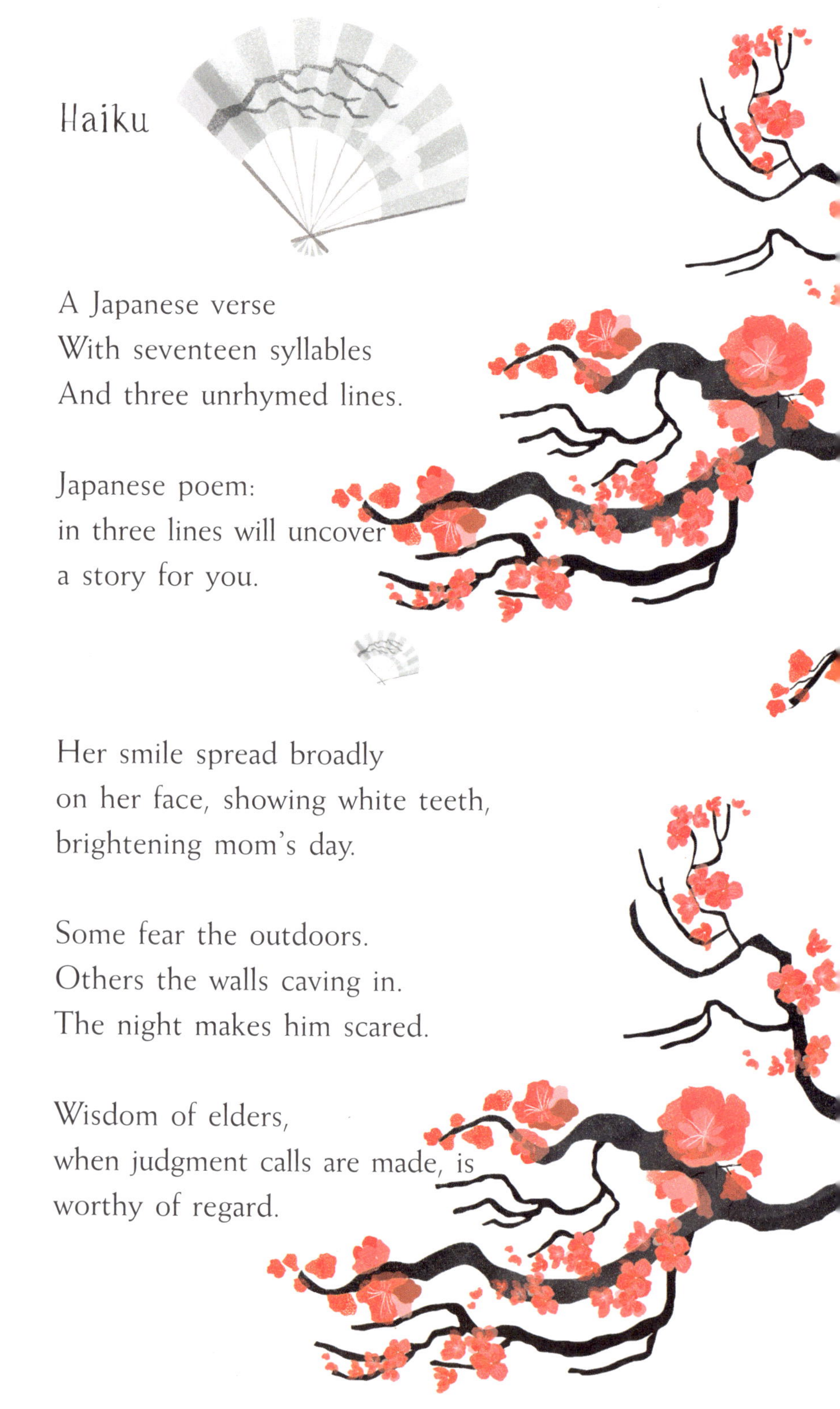

A Japanese verse
With seventeen syllables
And three unrhymed lines.

Japanese poem:
in three lines will uncover
a story for you.

Her smile spread broadly
on her face, showing white teeth,
brightening mom's day.

Some fear the outdoors.
Others the walls caving in.
The night makes him scared.

Wisdom of elders,
when judgment calls are made, is
worthy of regard.

Diamante

Diamante (one object)
Clever, creative (two adjectives about the object)
Building, making, showing (three verbs about the object)
Geometry, Poetry, Diamond, Stone (four nouns, two on this object and two on the next)
Shining, glowing, brightening (three verbs about the second object)
Brilliant, shapely (two adjectives about the second object)
Gem. (noun and second object)

Ice Cream/Salad

Ice Cream
cold, creamy
melting, dripping, dropping
confection, dessert, salad, vegetable
nourishing, strengthening, satisfying
crunchy, flavourful
Food!

An Acrostic Verse

An acrostic verse is fun to create,
Count the letters for lines: this one has eight.
Read and write the first letter
Or first word of each line.
So it describes it much better,
The word or phrase that you find.
It's a special form, whose message is clear
Creating a word as it's meant to appear.

Homework: the Dawdler's Lament

Homework can be such a chore
Often I lose my way.
My mind, it wanders here and there,
Each time I'd rather play!
Why must we always have to toil?
Or do our sums and read?
Recess all day will not spoil
Kids. More fun is what we need!

Limerick

The Limerick is a fun poem to pen.
Five lines reveal your acumen.
Two lines start the rhyme,
Then a couplet keeps time,
And the last line rhymes with the first, again.

There once was a poet named Lear
Who wrote lines of verse without fear,
Words of mischief he bared,
Tales of nonsense he shared,
And they laughed as they wiped off their tears.

I'll tell you a tale that's not long
Of a man who spoke only in song.
If you ask him the time
He replies with a chime
And it sounds like he said 'Ding-Dong'.

Nonets

Nonets take an unusual form. (9 syllables)
The first line has nine syllables (8 syllables)
The second line only eight. (7 syllables)
The third line just seven (6 syllables)
The fourth only six (5 syllables)
The fifth has five (4 syllables)
The sixth four (3 syllables)
And on (2 syllables)
End (1 syllable).

My Friend

Your loving hug wipes away my tears
Your smile makes me smile back as well.
When I'm alone, if you're there
Things seem so much better.
Friends are not just fun.
They brighten days.
They fill hours.
And bring.
Joy.

Villanelle

A Villanelle has nineteen lines.
In six stanzas lines divide.
In five, three-line verses the poem aligns.

Then in last four lines a couplet assigns.
Repetitions make words collide.
A Villanelle has nineteen lines.

Lines one and three repeat, refines,
Eight lines, through the poem wide.
In five, three-line (tercets) the poem aligns.

Same words echoed throughout show signs,
The poet's intent emphasized.
A Villanelle has nineteen lines.

With set rhyme scheme the words make designs,
And with set format sounds provide.
In tercets and one quatrain aligns.

To write this poem what are the signs?
Look to these words as guide.
A Villanelle in nineteen aligns,
Like a dancing song are the poem's lines.

Skipping Rope Song

Skipping rope, skipping rope—how wonderful this feels.
You lift my feet just off the ground,
The kids applaud my zeal.

My legs jump high as the rope wheels.
In fingers taut the rope is wound
Skipping rope, skipping rope—how wonderful this feels.

Skipping rope, skipping rope—this sport has much appeal
With cheers my twirling form they sound.
The kids applaud my zeal.

This kind of fun is just ideal
I jump up and down, my joy unbound
Skipping rope, skipping rope—how wonderful this feels.

Skipping rope, skipping rope—this sport has much appeal
Some make baskets to be crowned
But I'm skipping queen—huge deal!

The school kids never ever keel.
With ropes she plays and kicks her heel.
Skipping rope, skipping rope—your wonder I reveal.
Skipping rope, skipping rope—how wonderful this feels.

Couplet

A couplet is two lines of poetry.
Both lines should rhyme and share symmetry.

Even when they're on their own,
They have a musical tone.

But can close a longer poem,
Even bring the ending home.

A Reverie in Couplets

When I grow up, I want to be,
A painter, a potter, a poet, all three!

I'll paint large murals of fire and smoke,
Green plants, blue skies, and a gnarly, brown oak.

Tall goblets I'll craft, and big bowls of clay.
Smart words, and rhyme schemes—my poems on display!

To purchase my canvas, they'll come from afar
Will watch me do work. I'll be a superstar!

My verse in the books, my face on the page,
My name in the lights, at such a young age!

But textbooks are open, and homework's not done.
Sigh!... Still one day my art will be number one!

Triolet

A triolet is not three lines, but eight
And the first line occurs three times.
Line One is also Line Four, please just wait.
A triolet is not three lines, but eight.
The last two lines and the first two are mates.
And that's how a triolet rhymes!
A triolet is not three lines, but eight
And the first line occurs three times.

Baby Blues

I have a little brother and they brought him home today.
I thought he'd be fun, that he'd be my best friend.
His face is scrunched! His eyes are shut! He's bald,
but 'has to stay?'
I have a little brother and they brought him home today.
He only sleeps and cries all day. I wish he'd go away!
He doesn't do anything! His wails don't end!
I have a little brother and they brought him home today.
I thought he'd be fun, that he'd be my best friend.

So we've seen a few FORMS,
And we've worked out some RHYME.
We now know the norms,
And how rhythm keeps time.
Let's take what we've read; have a good look around.
Write our world in new verses, fresh forms that abound.
We'll see how far the English language can go.
Learning is such fun. Poems even more so!

Animal Groups

The English language has interesting nouns
For the groups of animals in fields and towns.
Of a herd of cows, you all have heard,
And a flock of chickens is not so absurd.
And a school of fish looks like it would please,
A teacher's class, or a gaggle of geese.

Yes, the English language has wonderful nouns
For the groups of animals in fields and towns.
A pride of lions rule the grassland.
And a murder of crows is a noisy band.
But a congress of baboons, even with wise jowls,
Will never outwit a parliament of owls.

The English language has outstanding nouns
For the groups of animals in fields and towns.
An exaltation of doves sounds divine,
But a crash of rhinos would get out of line!
A cloud of bats may lead to a frenzy,
And a swarm of bees?—Move away slowly.

Yes, English has some remarkable nouns
For the groups of animals in fields or towns.
A litter of puppies melts our hearts,
And a pit of snakes slithers and darts
A pack of wolves would bring to their knees,
A tower of giraffes that run and wheeze.

The English language has sensational nouns
For the groups of animals in fields or towns.
An army of caterpillars march in place.
A troop of kangaroos hop with grace.
A colony of ants build a large fort,
And a pod of dolphins frolic by the port.

Yes, the English language has enjoyable nouns
For the groups of animals in fields or towns.
Pearls can't be found in a bed of clams,
But a family of beavers will treasure their dams.
Boy the animal kingdom is so replete,
And with human beings is clearly complete!

Cheese Can Please

Let's travel the world and choose us some cheese:
Camembert from high mountains. Maybe Feta from Greece?
Hard, yellow Gruyere favoured by the Swiss,
From the French—a strong cheese—the Roquefort, don't miss.
Mozzarella from Italy makes pasta sooo good.
Soft paneer from India is put in curries for food.
Which cheese would YOU pick if YOU were to choose?
English or New York Cheddar? Let us peruse.
Bleu Cheese, so chunky, from the United States
Savoury French Brie for my clamouring mates!
Or the nutty, firm cheese from Holland: Edam.
But for me, it's the mild Gouda that goes nicely with ham.
We call it Swiss cheese, Emmental full of holes.
German Limburger's great too, if you just hold your nose...
Which cheese would YOU pick if YOU were to choose?

Hard? Yellow? Soft? Served with fruit? In fondue?
Let's travel the world to find us some cheese.
Take your pick from this list, or any others you please!

Onomatopoeia

What is this strange word, I wonder,
With vowels all jumbled together?
Listen to me, and I'll tell you—
Said my cousin, the teacher, Parmender.

If horses' hooves should go *cloppity clop clop*
You can hear the sound of their trot.
And if the rain coming down *pitters* and *patters*
That's precisely its sound—is it not?

Well then *cloppity clop clop,* and *pitter* and *patter*
Are words whose sound can be heard.
So 'onomatopoeia' in poems,
Is the formation and use of such words.

Woof Woof, Bang Bang, Buzz, and *Cackle*
Clatter and *Hiss* and *Zoom*
Twitter and *Sizzle* and *Murmur*
And can't you just hear the sound of a *Boom*?

The formation and use of such words
That imitate the sound that they name
Is onomatopoeia in Greek language,
Use the term and you can take the path to fame!

Hello World!

Jambo is 'hello' in Swahili,
In Kenya that's how people come and go.
Namaste is 'hello' in Hindi,
In India we may greet each other so.

Bonjour chirp the French every morning,
Guten Tag is what the Germans say.
Konnichiwa, is a Japanese expression—
Wishing everyone a pleasant day!

If you happen to speak Hungarian,
Sziastok, is what you'd say if friends come near.
If in Spain you find yourself sometime,
Just say *Hola*, do not fear.

In Hawaii, we'll shout *Aloha*
In China, *Ni Hao* will do the trick.
And if our travels take us far,
As-salaam-a'alaykum is Arabic.

So, when around the world you wander,
And hope to greet the ones you meet,
You'll know what they say in their language
And friendship will be an easy feat!

Mothering

My mother wears a sari, his mother: a sarong.
Some mothers like a pretty skirt, that's either short or long.
A caftan loose and flowing in Middle East is worn.
The salwaar, just like trousers, gives comfort, night and morn.
In Germany, some mothers wear the dirndl, gracefully.
With bodice, blouse, and apron, that falls from waist to knee.
The rebozo's just a piece of cloth, but worn many different ways.
In Mexico, moms wrap and shade their babies from the sun's hot rays.
Ethiopians cover heads and shoulders with a handmade netela.
In rain or shine, most mothers have no need for an umbrella!
The Navajo and Hopi use mantas in their weddings.
This useful dress or blanket can make a comfy bedding!

So fitted pants or dresses, kimono, or culottes,
With silk or frilly flounces, with sashes, bows, or knots,
What mothers wear don't matter, they love us just the same;
And when they hold us in their arms, their clothing has no name.

Houses and Homes

Sun dried brick houses of the desert,
Wood frame houses in Tennessee,
Tepees of the Native Americans,
My sister likes her playhouse on a tree.
Ice houses, called igloos, are so cool!
Inuits make their home in such a place.
Reed houses in swampy water,
Some dwellings are in a jungle's maze.
Stone houses of faraway China,
Underground houses in basement floors,
Painted houses of brick and mortar,
With bamboo, or hardwood doors.
Houses of straw that can be carried,
Clay houses, built like earthenware,
Bungalows, with green lawns and terrace,
Chalets and grand castles that make you stare!
Cottages, cabins, houseboats, and trailers too,
All houses become a home, when it's occupied by
love and YOU!

Welcome Home

There are so many houses that you could live in,
If you're looking for 'home', where would you begin?

In the desert are structures of sun-dried clay.
Log cabins are built of wood.
There are tepees made from cloth and skins,
I'd live in a tree house, if I could.
Some dwellings can be made from reeds or straw.
Inuits build igloos of ice.
Some homes are made of stone or brick,
Floating houseboats are a paradise!
Some houses have attics with spiders and webs,
Some houses have basement floors,
Some homes reach up four stories high!
Some homes are completely outdoors!
Some homes are made in grand old castles.
Some people reside in hotels.
There are houses with gardens, and big green lawns
There are homes in big cities as well.

Yes, there are many houses to build and live in,
Home is where you're welcome, wherever you've been.

Living Situations

I live at home with Mami and Pa.
Gita lives with both her Dads.
Henry goes back and forth each week,
Between his parents' pads.

Jose lives with his Abuela;
She takes him everywhere.
Ivy and Lily stay with fathers,
When they're not in daycare.

Everyone's family is unique,
And different from all the rest.
For when a home is full of love and cheer,
that family is blessed.

April Fool's Day

There's one day a year, when children are free,
To do as they wish, and do as they please.
With vigour and verve on April Fool's Day,
We can trick anyone, and still get away!
We can put glue on doorknobs, and paint on the floor,
Can tie shoelaces together, and laugh with uproar!
Can add sweet to the soup, and salt to the tea,
And when glares come our way, we can say 'wasn't me!'
But Maya put ink on the teacher's big chair,
And Sonali found chewing gum in her long hair.
Now teacher has taken our playtime away,
I guess April's big 'trick' is on us kids for today!